# MY BEST PRACTICE: PROGRAMS VS SERVICES

Matt Bratlien and G.L. Dart

net-tech

Acronyms:
MSP: Managed Service Provider
PTO: Professional Technology Organization

ISBN: 978-1-7333519-5-9 (Print edition)
ISBN: 978-1-7333519-6-6 (Kindle/ebook edition)

Illustration by Michael Rohani. Book Design by DesignforBooks.com

Printed in the United States

DOES SHE WORK HERE?
THAT'S MY PERSONAL TRAINER, AMY.
SHE HAS HER OWN PROGRAM,
BUT WE COME HERE TO TRAIN.

WHY NOT WORK OUT ON YOUR OWN?
I TRIED USING THE GYM'S SERVICES
BUT DIDN'T SEE RESULTS OR HIT MY GOALS.

THEN I SAW A FLYER FOR AMY'S PROGRAM,
AND THAT'S WHEN IT CLICKED.
WHAT CLICKED?

CLASS SCHEDULE
THE DIFFERENCE BETWEEN A PROGRAM AND A SERVICE.
THEY AREN'T THE SAME?
NO, BUT PEOPLE USE THOSE TERMS INTERCHANGEABLY.

CLASS SCHEDULE
AND NONE OF THESE CLASSES ARE PROGRAMS?
NO. THEY'RE ANOTHER EXAMPLE OF A SERVICE.

PROGRAMS ARE ACTIONABLE PLANS THAT ADDRESS SPECIFIC ISSUES AND NEEDS.
THEY ARE DESIGNED TO EFFECT POSITIVE CHANGE.

HOW?
PROGRAMS SET CLEAR OBJECTIVES THAT CAN BE MEASURED.
AND CREATE A PATH TO SUCCESS.

SO HOW DOES AMY HELP?
I WORK WITH AMY TO GET THE CHANGE I WANT.
IS THAT *REALLY* WORTH IT?
PROGRAMS, LIKE AMY'S, PROVIDE MORE THAN A PLAN.

OFFICES
ACCOUNTABILITY IS BUILT IN.
WHOEVER RUNS THE PROGRAM IS RESPONSIBLE FOR RESULTS,
AND PROGRESS IS MEASURABLE.

OFFICES
WHY DOES THAT MATTER?
IF I TELL AMY I'M NOT SEEING RESULTS FROM HER PROGRAM
SHE LISTENS, TAKES RESPONSIBILITY, AND ADJUSTS THE PLAN.

MANAGEMENT
COULDN'T YOU COMPLAIN TO THE GYM?
NO, THE GYM IS A "SERVICE" WITH TOOLS
BUT ISN'T ACCOUNTABLE FOR RESULTS.

WHY NOT?
SERVICES ARE BENEFICIAL ACTIVITIES
BUT THEY AREN'T DESIGNED WITH CHANGE OR ACCOUNTABILITY IN MIND.

DOES THAT MAKE SERVICES BAD?
NO, BUT THEY AREN'T ALWAYS EFFECTIVE.

THEY CAN BE BENEFICIAL TO THE PERSON USING THEM
BUT THERE IS NO STRUCTURE.
CHANGE MIGHT OCCUR,
BUT IT MIGHT NOT.

BUT PROGRAMS LEAD TO CHANGE?
YES. THEY'RE INTENTIONALLY DESIGNED
TO GET RESULTS FOR ORGANIZATIONS.

HOW DOES THE PERSON RUNNING THE PROGRAM KNOW YOU'RE ON TRACK?
THEY TAKE BASELINE MEASUREMENTS,
AND REGULARLY MONITOR INDICATORS TO CHECK YOUR PROGRESS.

COULDN'T YOU SET UP YOUR OWN TRACKING SYSTEM
AND DESIGN YOUR OWN PROGRAM?
THAT'S WHAT I TRIED BEFORE AMY.
IT DIDN'T WORK.

I'M NOT A FITNESS EXPERT.
I USED THE GYM'S SERVICES RANDOMLY,
NOT KNOWING WHICH ACTIVITIES WERE RIGHT FOR MY GOALS.

PROGRAMS KNOW WHICH ACTIVITIES ARE RIGHT?
YES. PEOPLE USE PROGRAMS TO GET RESULTS THEY ARE LOOKING FOR.
THEY ARE CAREFULLY DESIGNED BY EXPERTS,
WHO KNOW HOW TO REACH GOALS.

THERE'S NO STRUCTURE TO SERVICES.
YOU CANNOT EFFECTIVELY CREATE CHANGE
OR TRACK RESULTS TO A PARTICULAR ACTIVITY WITH SERVICES.
YOU MIGHT NOT EVEN GET RESULTS!

ARE THERE OTHER EXAMPLES OF PROGRAMS?
YES!
AT WORK WE USE ONE FOR OUR I.T. SYSTEMS.

HOW DOES THAT WORK?
IT'S CALLED AN I.T. SUBSCRIPTION PROGRAM.

YOGA CLASS
THERE'S NO DECISION MAKING.
ALL OUR I.T. EQUIPMENT AND TOOLS ARE PROVIDED,
AND EVERY CLIENT USES THE SAME PROCESSES.

YOGA CLASS
HOW DOES USING THE SAME PROCESSES
AS EVERYONE ELSE
HELP YOUR COMPANY?

PROGRAMS ARE STRENGTHENED BY PARTICIPANTS.
WHEN A BETTER WAY IS DISCOVERED,
IT'S APPLIED ACROSS THE BOARD
AND EVERYONE BENEFITS, NOT JUST MY COMPANY.

DO CHANGES LIKE THAT COST EXTRA?
NO, THE I.T. SUBSCRIPTION PROGRAM CHARGES A FLAT FEE.
EVERYTHING IS INCLUDED, EVEN THOSE UPGRADES,
AND WE MAKE FEWER DECISIONS.

UNCLE TONY WORKS IN I.T.
DOES HE HAVE AN I.T. SUBSCRIPTION PROGRAM?
NO, UNCLE TONY IS A MANAGED SERVICE PROVIDER (MSP).

YEAH! HE OFFERS *MANAGED* SERVICES.
DOES THAT MEAN IT'S A PROGRAM?
NO, MSPs ARE LIKE THE GYM.

MSPs SELL SERVICES AND SUPPORT PACKAGES.
FEW THINGS ARE STANDARDIZED, SO CHANGE CAN'T
BE MEASURED LIKE IN STRUCTURED PROGRAMS.
OH.

DID YOU EVER USE AN MSP?
YES. IT DIDN'T WORK FOR US,
AND WAS INCREDIBLY STRESSFUL.

WHY?
IF SOMETHING WENT WRONG
OUR MSP WOULD SAY
IT WAS BECAUSE WE DIDN'T FOLLOW THEIR GUIDANCE.

THAT DOESN'T SOUND FAIR.
MSPs ARE EXPERTS.
SHOULDN'T THEY DO MORE?

IT'S NOT THEIR BUSINESS MODEL
TO MAKE DECISIONS FOR CLIENTS.
BECAUSE THEY ONLY PROVIDE SERVICES?

YES, YOU'RE STARTING TO SEE THE DIFFERENCE!
BUT UNCLE TONY ALWAYS HELPS ME.
HE *REALLY* DOESN'T DO MORE FOR HIS CUSTOMERS?

MSPs LIKE UNCLE TONY LOOK AT EACH COMPANY SEPARATELY.
THEN THEY MAKE RECOMMENDATIONS AND SELL PROJECTS BASED ON THE KNOWLEDGE OF THE TECHNICIAN.
MENU

MENU
IS THAT BAD?
YES, BECAUSE MSPs CAN'T KEEP THE STANDARDS MY PROGRAM HAS.
AND THAT INTRODUCES RISKS FOR THEIR CUSTOMERS.

MENU
RISK OF WHAT?
MAKING THE WRONG DECISION.

WHAT DO YOU MEAN?
MSP CUSTOMERS MAKE ALL THEIR OWN DECISIONS,
BASED ON THE ADVICE OF ONE TECHNICIAN.
WHAT KIND OF DECISIONS?

WHAT HARDWARE AND SOFTWARE THEY WANT.
WHEN TO UPGRADE.
WHICH CYBERSECURITY TOOLS TO DEPLOY.
THE LIST GOES ON.

EXIT
THAT SOUNDS LIKE IT TAKES A LOT OF TIME.
IT DID. AND IT WAS STRESSFUL.
IF WE MADE THE WRONG CHOICE,
IT PUT *OUR* COMPANY AT RISK. *NOT THE MSP.*

AND THAT DOESN'T HAPPEN NOW?
EXIT
NOPE! OUR I.T. SUBSCRIPTION PROGRAM IS RUN BY OUR PROFESSIONAL TECHNOLOGY ORGANIZATION (PTO).
THEY DECIDE FOR US BASED ON BEST PRACTICE.

EXIT
EVERYTHING IS STANDARDIZED.
IT'S THEIR SYSTEMS, EQUIPMENT, AND PROCESSES WE USE.
IF SOMETHING BREAKS, THEY REPLACE IT.
IF RESULTS AREN'T HAPPENING, THEY HAVE TO ADDRESS IT.

THEIR I.T. SUBSCRIPTION PROGRAM PROVIDES A PATH FOR US.
IT'S NOT OUR DECISIONS OR ACTIONS.
OUR PTO EVEN BUYS AND REPLACES EVERYTHING
WHEN NEW DEVICES ARE RELEASED.

WE WANTED SOMEONE
TO BE ACCOUNTABLE FOR OUR RESULTS.
SO NOW YOU CAN FOCUS ON YOUR BUSINESS?
YES, AND HOW TO USE I.T. TO HELP ACHIEVE OUR GOALS.

THANKS FOR EXPLAINING THE DIFFERENCES. I THINK I GET IT.
YOU DO?
YEAH. MANAGED SERVICE PROVIDERS (MSPs) AREN'T ACCOUNTABLE FOR YOUR CHANGE OR RESULTS.

BUT YOUR PROFESSIONAL TECHNOLOGY ORGANIZATION (PTO) MAKES ALL DECISIONS.
THEY'LL FIX WHAT'S WRONG
AND ADJUST IF YOUR BUSINESS DOESN'T SEE RESULTS.

EXACTLY! AN I.T. SUBSCRIPTION PROGRAM PROVIDES OUTCOMES.
NOT A RANDOM SET OF ACTIVITIES.
AND LESS RISK.

YOU KNOW WHAT I'M WAITING FOR?
WHAT'S THAT?
AN ICE CREAM SUBSCRIPTION PROGRAM!

## Why We're Committed to Helping Organizations with Technology

Although technology has changed dramatically since we started in the industry two decades ago, the frustration and waste associated with IT support remains.

Poorly defined expectations and an overall lack of standards make it challenging to compare IT strategies or see the true value of a technology partner. As we speak with local organizations, we continue to find unfavorable accounts surrounding inflated budgets and short-term fixes.

G.L. Dart

**We understand the frustration.**

Discussions like these do not align with the role we believe technology should play within an organization. Technology needs to be managed with a long-term, business-driven vision, not patchwork fixes. That's why we established the first Professional Technology Organization (PTO), a holistic IT solution designed to actually manage the data, not just react to issues, in our client's environments.

Matt Bratlien

Working with a PTO brings a true business partner to your team. We focus on aligning our IT expertise with your objectives to find the technologies and solutions that drive growth. Our thorough processes and systems are designed to bring scalable IT solutions to your organization.

—Matt Bratlien and G.L. (George) Dart, Net-Tech cofounders

MY BEST PRACTICE: PTO
Matt Bratlien and G.L. Dart

MY BEST PRACTICE: INFOSEC
Matt Bratlien and G.L. Dart

MY BEST PRACTICE:
PROGRAMS VS SERVICES
Matt Bratlien and G.L. Dart

Printed in the USA
CPSIA information can be obtained
at www.ICGtesting.com
CBHW081652120424
6731CB00005B/37

9 781733 351959